Healing Words

Also by Alexandra Vasiliu

Healing Is a Gift

Time to Heal

Dare to Let Go

Be My Moon

Blooming

Magnetic

Plant Hope

Through the Heart's Eyes

Healing Words

A Poetry Collection for Broken Hearts

Alexandra Vasiliu

Stairway Books
Boston

To all those with scars
in their hearts

Contents

Crashing

Military Decorations

When I was young,
I went to war
with the demons of youth.

I plunged headlong
into the front line.
I heard
the missiles
of disappointment
striking and colliding
next to me.

I saw my friends
left almost dead
in the pit of despair,
eyes wide open
in the darkness
of loneliness.

I felt hopeless.
I couldn't save anyone.
All I could do
was clench my teeth
and channel my will
into running away.

Oh, God,
how fast I ran
in those years.
I ran
like a crazy animal.

Sometimes
I thought
it wasn't me running
so frantically,
but instead
my desire to live.
I ran,
pushing my limits hard.
I ran
from youth's devils.
I ran
from fear, anxiety,
sadness, heartbreak,
and loneliness.

I ran
from death.
I ran in the space
between life and death.
My inner death.
I ran
like a hunted animal.
That was my solution.

But despite all my efforts,
eventually those demons
captured and beat me.
I remembered my friends
left behind
in the pit of despair
and I wept
for them
with all my heart.
The blood of my dreams
drowned my hopes.

"How will I ever see
the end of this war?
How will I ever rise again
from my heart's wounds?"
I asked myself.

I wanted to defeat
these demons—
not for my pride,
but to alleviate my pains
and to find peace.

"I want to live,"
I said to myself.
"I will stand up.
No matter how hard it is going to be,
I will stand up.
I am not afraid anymore.
My eyes are wide open
to see and understand
that I am alive
for one reason.
God entrusted me
with life and strength.
I need to survive
and win this war.
I will defeat these demons
with the arms
of patience,
goodness,
wisdom,
forgiveness,
and hope.

"No matter
how much these demons drag me
down,
I will fight to live
and to be merciful."

And that is precisely what I did.
Since then,
I wear my heart's scars
like military decorations
from a war
I fought hard and won.

Even now,
I still wake up imagining myself
running again
like a crazy animal.
Running
from youth's demons.
Running
from death.
My inner death.

But I touch my heart.

Immediately
I feel my scars,
my hidden military decorations.

I smile
and say to my heart,
"You are alive.
We won."

Solitude Is a Desert

Solitude is like crossing a desert.
No matter which way you turn your head,
no matter how far you run,
there is nobody around you.

No smiles,
no caring words
to quench
your thirst
for comfort and affection.

Just the sinking feeling
that this inner drought
will result in
the drying up
of your whole soul.

You pass through a desert.

Your desert.

You look around.

The desert is devoid
of fertility,
just as your heart is empty of life.

You are alone.

"Where to find hope?"
You pass through a desert.
Your desert—a sterile soil.

Suddenly,
an image flashes
through your mind.

Tiny flowers grow
even in the desert.

Maybe that is your hope too.

Nothing is in vain,
not even a dream.
Hold a beautiful image
in your heart
like you would hold a flower
in your hands.
You will feel less lonely.

What a Tiger!

Has anyone ever told you
loneliness is a wild animal
that never sleeps
and is always hunting for food?

Inside your heart,
I hear
a tiger roaring.

Don't fear this beast.
The tiger of loneliness will break down
all your inner barriers
and knock you to the ground.
It will cleave your heart
with claws of pain.
It will shred
every part of your soul.
Not one of your hopes,
not one of your thoughts,

not one of your feelings
will be spared.

You will scream.
You will cry.
You will hope for rescue
while you feel
the tiger's maw
devouring every piece
of your heart.
You will fight
until this beast leaves you
half dead along the road.

"Oh, cruel tiger,
how I want you
to never find a heart
to your liking!
How I want you
to starve
until the end of the days!
Oh, tiger of loneliness,
how I pray
for the moment
when you retreat
from this world.
I know that one day,

you will die.
"You will be a mere memory.
You will be forgotten
like a fossil
gathering dust
in a museum.
The world will be too bright
to host you.
One day,
love will heal all people's hearts.
Oh, cruel tiger,
you are nothing.
One day,
you will find out."

Despite this fight,
you will get up,
because you are strong.
And you will have one thing
to do.
Pray to meet a soulful person
who can soothe
your heart.

Slowly Fading

Beneath my skin,
loneliness sparks like a fire.
I am stuck inside a cage.
My heart.
My mind.
My body.
I want to run away,
but it is in vain.
The flames are too strong
and I am surrounded by fears.
Sometimes,
loneliness burns down
every positive thought.
I am slowly fading,
wishing to save my heart's dreams.

A Dead City

Your past is a dead city.
Stop letting
its ruins haunt you.

Don't fear, though.
Your past can't ever catch up
with you.

You are the only survivor.

Get up
and head straight
to the launch of a new beginning.

Touch the horizon of hopes;
it holds a promise
for something else,
for a better start,
for a new tomorrow.

Don't push back.
Remember,
your past is a dead city.

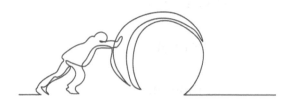

From now on,
you will thrive
at whatever you choose.

Don't choose your past anymore,
because your past life is dead
and death has nothing to offer.

Choose life.
It will bring you the gift of love.

Loneliness Is a Snake

Loneliness is a snake
that slithers so deep under your skin,
its venom easily poisons
your heart and mind.

This creature crawls crookedly
in your veins,
in your blood,
in your emotions.

This ophidian reptile sucks
every bit of your energy,
painfully consuming your life.

Loneliness is a venomous snake
that spews deadly bitterness
in your heart and mind.
It is very skilled at bringing tears
to your eyes.

Will you be brave enough
to fight it?
Will you be able to free your feelings
from its deadly grip?

Take a deep breath.

You can yet rally.
The fire of life still burns
in the depths of your heart.

In the Middle of the City

Have you ever recognized
lonely people
in the middle of the city?
They always go out
when it rains.
They always "forget" their umbrellas.
They walk for hours,
while the wind snarls their hair
and steals their thoughts.
Their hearts cry out,
craving affection.

Rain is their perfect mask.

Lonely people let their tears
mingle with raindrops.

How strange
it is for them

to seek therapy
in the middle of the city.

How sad
it is for them
to know
that nobody will ever notice
the lake of tears
they left behind
in the rain.

Magnifying Glasses

Solitude gives you a magnifying glass
to help see yourself better.

It's a spiritual activity.

You become self-aware.
You see yourself metaphysically
blind,
ill,
bitter,
selfish,
arrogant,
heartless,
and in so many other different ways.

But you don't have to
buy into
self-defeating thoughts.

You are more than that.
You are much more
than your wounds.

Work on your heart
in order to be
a kind person,
easy to love,
and impossible to leave.

Hope Is Like a Rope

An older man once told me,
"Hope is like a rope."

Oh, he didn't have a clue
how much I needed
this rope,
in order to scale
the mountains of my afflictions,
and to find a vantage point
where I could see
the horizon of a new life.

"Where can I find this rope, sir?"

"Oh, it is simple.
The first thing you should do
is imprint two words
upon your heart.
Let go.

"Let go of worries.
Let go of fears.
Let go of all dark thoughts.
Let go of anything
that is toxic or unnecessary.
Let go is the beginning of all hopes.
And you can find this rope
within yourself first."

Growing Up

On my way home,
I saw some graffiti
which read,

I have never changed.

Oh, what sad words
that stabbed a knife
in my heart.

Tears streamed down my cheeks.

"You who wrote these words,
you are alone,"
I said to myself.
"You are alone,
for nobody can stay
with a person
who never changes.

"You are alone,
for nobody can find support
in a person
who never grows up.
Oh, you who wrote these words,
I wish you
find love
and change yourself."

Then,
I came closer to that graffiti
and added one more line:

. . . until I met you.

Plant a Healing Word

On the place
where someone broke
your heart,
plant
a healing word,
like you would seed
a flower.

Water it
with your wisdom.

Nurture it
with your resilience.

Cover its body
with a blanket of hope.

Let it grow.

One day,
this tiny healing word
will bloom
in your heart
and change you
into a flower.

In that moment,
you will be
ready for love.

Another Continent

When you are a teenager,
you travel
through an unknown continent.

Everything waits for you
to be discovered.

Somehow
you are like Adam
in the garden of paradise,
with the gift to name
every feeling,
every emotion,
every mood
once again.

When you are a teenager,
start naming everything
like it was never christened before.

Create everything afresh.
Give birth to a new world
from your heart.

Give rise to a beautiful world.
Your world.
Word by word,
let everything take the shape
of your dreams.
Life.
Love.
Peace.
Happiness.

Retain your awe and wonder.
This is the way to live
when you are a teenager.

Not an Alien

Sometimes when you wake up
or when you go about your day
or when you return home,
you ask yourself,
"Where do I belong?"
You feel lost and empty.
You feel utterly alone.

Sometimes,
you are envious of those
who are comfortable
with themselves.
They don't ask questions,
even if their lives have
no perfect answers.

Other times,
you are jealous of those
who have found their soul mates.

At last, they have
a sense of belonging
and their hearts are safe.

"Where do I fit in?"
you ask yourself
every time
you feel you have missed out on
an essential meaning of life.

You feel utterly alone.

Although, let me tell you
that loneliness is not
your final destination.

An empty heart
is not your nature.

You are not an alien.
This world was also made
for you.
Stick to this truth,
despite your insecurity.

Heal your heart
with these words:

"The world waits for me too.
The world has gifts for me too."

You are not an alien.
Do not succumb
to your fears.

Move on.

Loneliness is not
your final destination.

You deserve love.
You deserve joy.
You deserve life.

Every time
you ask yourself,
"Where do I fit in?"
say to your soul,
"I deserve love.
I am a gift to this world.
And one day,
I will be a gift of love
for someone
who will love me too."

The Life's Seed

If your heart is in disarray,
your life will have the same pattern.
You will have dark thoughts
and bad experiences,
then need to deal with
lingering feelings after
sailing through rivers of tears
from toxic relationships.

If your heart is in disarray,
the blizzards of loneliness
will blow
into your life
sooner or later.
You will be left devastated
like a house
that has lost
its windows and doors.

Where should you start
rebuilding
your life?

How can you bring
strength and coherence
in your heart?

Is there a miraculous seed for that?

Hold on to your dreams.

Don't wait in
a pool of stagnant tears.

Find a seed of hope
and plant it deep down
in your heart.

One day,
you will bloom again.

Tell Me
Some Healing Words

Maybe the sea was never green
and the sky was never blue.

Maybe the ocean was never deep
and the mountains were never high.

Maybe the days were never bright
and the nights were never dark.

Maybe everybody was right,
except me.

In the end, what did it matter?

I needed some healing words.

Either in the sea or the sky.

Either in the ocean
or in the mountains.

Either in the brightness of days
or in the darkness of nights.

Some healing words
to comfort me,
to soothe my broken heart.

Some healing words
to connect again
with my soul.

The sea, the sky, the ocean,
the mountains, the days, the nights;
the whole universe
whispers into my ears,
"You are not alone."

Maybe this is the only truth
I can take on my journey.

Maybe these are the only healing words
I will ever hear.

I am not alone.
I am not alone.
I am not alone.
I am not alone.

The whole creation of God is here
for me
as a gift,
as a friend.

And if I am not alone,
remember you are not alone either,
whoever you are,
wherever you are.

A Pair of Us

If my heart is broken
and yours is too,
then that makes us a pair
and we could do something together.
We could hang around each other
and tell our life stories.
We could sigh together,
hope or laugh at ourselves.
Or we could bathe
in the river of our tears.
Broken hearts
need to be cleansed of all pains.
Nevertheless,
we could let peace infuse our souls.
Or together we could grasp
the magic needle
that sews and repairs
the holes of our hearts.

If my heart is broken
and yours is too,
don't be afraid.
That makes us a pair
and we can do something together.

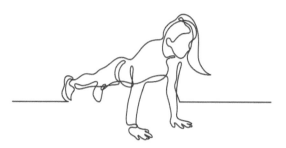

Crawling

Silence

I feel a heavy silence
taking over my heart.
I can't pierce it.
No knife exists
that can go so deep.
All I want is to stop loneliness
from creeping into my heart
and to live my life again.
Though, I know that I have to pay
for this kind of freedom.
Becoming whole
is not without its price.

Alone

I write
from my wounds
and let my pain flow
like ink.
I scream
with my mouth closed
and let my words spread
on paper
like a river of tears.
This is the way to save me
from all the inner chaos
and let go.
Sometimes, writing is therapy.

Difficult Lessons

I will not lie to you.

As time passes,
you will learn to suffer.

You will learn
how heartbreak feels,
how loss tastes,
and what loneliness brings
into your heart.

You will learn
to bury your tears,
your pains,
your failures,
and your unfulfillments
into deep graves
and never look back.

You will survive many near-deaths
of your soul,
but you must stand up,
overcome your heart's wounds,
and go on with your life.

Choose yourself.
Start forgetting sad things
that once seemed unforgettable.
Forgive cruel things
that once seemed unforgivable.
Start healing your thoughts,
so that you will find peace.
Replace the desert in your heart
with flowery gardens of kindness.
There is no other way
to move on with your life.
Meaning comes
through careful reflection
after suffering.
But remember
that despite what you go through
in life,
you will always be
worthy of true love.

Get Out of Here

Inside your chest
lives a little nightingale
who never sleeps.

When dark thoughts surround you,
the little bird starts telling you,
"Young woman,
those thoughts will lead you
to the forest of depression.
Do not cross its boundaries.
There you will find no truth about yourself.
Run.
Run away.
Run as fast as you can.
Even if you have to run
through valleys,
over hills and mountains,
or if you have to face ghosts,
just run.

"Don't stop.
Run, heading
only for light."

Then the little nightingale adds,
"Don't let depression swallow you.
Don't waste your time.
Make your life an ascent
toward love and light."

Young woman,
let the little nightingale sing
inside your chest.

Let it always remind you
that you can go
anywhere you want,
even if some places deeply harm you.

All the dark forests of this life
have powerful voices
to beckon you,
but nothing good to offer.

Do not listen to them.

Do not follow them.

Soak up all the love
of kind people around you
and make something beautiful
with your life.

Beautiful Again

Even if I am heartbroken
or have puffy eyes
from crying,
could you tell me, please,
that I am still beautiful?
I will feel relieved,
as though you have seeded hope
in my sad heart.

The Tiny Jail

Loneliness makes you feel
like a prisoner caged in jail.
You long for a shift in mood
as a captive wishes to stroll
in a quiet, sunny place.

"How can I free myself?
How can I prevail?"
you ask yourself.

Let me tell you the way.

Loneliness leads you
to think only of yourself.

You are not
the only prisoner caged
in a tiny cell.

So if you want to conquer
this dark storm,
go and help others.

To be alone is a form of enslavement.
Stop being enslaved.
Be a healer.
Be generous.

Give your love away.
And you will be free forever.

Still Yearning for Love

If you feel heartbroken,
take a stroll
in the sun.
A broken heart always needs
to be mended with light.

On a Wild Ocean

Loneliness is like sailing
on a wild, furious ocean.

Two fragile oars
are your only tools
for returning to shore.
Your reflections
and your prayers
are your only company.

"Will I be a good sailor?
Will I be able
to calm down
the madness of this ocean?"
you keep thinking.

Now start praying for solid land,
where thoughts can't sink you,
where vulnerability doesn't exist,
where sadness doesn't persist,
where love is a constant feeling.

Pray. Imagine that.
Dream of it.
And keep rowing,
heading straight ahead.

Somewhere there must be a shore.
And this can be a new beginning.

Run Away

My inner voice once screamed at me,
"Run! Run away!
You need people around you.
You need love.
Run! Run away
from the land of ghosts.
Loneliness won't make you feel
worthy of life."

I listened to that voice.

I ran as fast as I could.

With every step I took,
my heart became a little bit lighter.

Looking only at the horizon,
I had hope.

"Maybe
somewhere,
sometime,
somehow,
something good waits for me too."

Isolation

When life seems to be
an empty glass
in which you scream alone,
your voice returns
with an echo to say,
"Everything is absurd."

You ask yourself,
"Is there any meaning
to so much loneliness,
to so much sadness,
to so much nothingness?"

Let me tell you,
life is not a riddle.
What if your pain is not in vain?

Don't back yourself into a corner.

Step up to fight.
In the end,
you must gather the courage to live
with the answer you receive.

You are merely
a blank piece of paper
in God's hands.

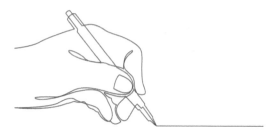

Listen to how destiny's pencil
inscribes the parchment of your heart.
And follow your calling.

Necessary Skills

If you want to free yourself
from the void of loneliness,
you must learn
the skills of an architect.
Learn to build bridges
of light and love
from your heart
to the hearts of others.

Alexandra Vasiliu

Heavy Luggage

Loneliness comes into your life
like heavy luggage.
The weight of feeling depressed,
heartbroken,
unhappy,
scared,
hopeless,
lost,
and abandoned.
The weight of feeling frozen
in a living body.
Oh, how many times
you wished
to have a heart
several pounds lighter!
How many times
you wished
to shake off
loneliness

like a dog shakes
water from its fur!
How many times
you wished
to easily fly
like a simple bird!
How many times
you imagined yourself weightless
like the sigh of a newborn!
So why don't you get rid of
this heavy luggage?
Open your heart
and let go of all the chains
keeping you tethered to the ground.
Feel the blessing
of being alive,
living life,
and building dreams.
At the end of the day,
nobody wants to be burdened with
a massive piece of luggage,
yet the dream remains
to easily fly like a simple bird.

Ghosts

When you remember
painful things from your past
and when you feel
empty,
lonely,
or heartbroken,
don't run.

Look into the eyes
of those memories
and declare,
"Don't visit me anymore.
I don't belong to you.
I belong to love."

A Gift So Simple

Look at my heart's wounds
like you would gaze upon
an unknown landscape.

Don't be afraid
to enter my heart.

All I want from you
is for you to save my heart
from loneliness
and show me how worthy of love
I am.

Show me how much you love me.

This is how I will be cured
of my loneliness.

Even if you have to climb
the jagged mountains of my scars
or to swim
the ocean of my bitter tears,
please don't give up.

Show me your love.

Look at my heart's wounds
and say,
"My love will heal you,
for only love can heal
and restore any life."

A Path to Your Heart

When loneliness stings
your soul
and suffering becomes
second nature,
remember that
this is life's experience.

This is the way of becoming
a grown-up.

Maturing is not about uneasiness
or being alone.

Maturing is about understanding
your limits
and becoming
a hero.
Your hero.

Turn your pains into wisdom.

One day,
you will be able
to save your heart,
along with many others.

Show Me

When I was drowning in despair,
I found no better escape
than the belief that one day,
someone would say to me,
"My love,
show me all your wounds and tears.
I will kneel and kiss every pain
that broke your heart.
I will kneel and touch every tear
that washed away your hope.
I will kneel and heal
every blow you received.
I will shower you with kisses.
I am here only for you.
I am here, in your life, only to love you."

Something Else

You know
that there is much more
than loneliness
in your heart.

Something mysterious,
something powerful,
something deep in your thoughts.

You know it
and feel it,
even if you can't name it.

Maybe it is the hope
that one day
you can be the sun of love
for someone.

Maybe
it is the condition of being human,
despite the cruelty
of those who broke your heart.

There is much more
than loneliness
in your heart.

There is something else,
something magnificent
that whispers,
"You will hope again.
You will live again.
You will love again."

Such a Simple Way

Whatever you have been through,
one day
your journey
through loneliness
will end.

You'll find the will
to live again,
to change yourself
and make beautiful wishes,
to get along with friends
and kind people,
to give all your love away,
to shoot an arrow of hope
and aim for a dream.

One day,
your heart will feel young and bold
again.

You will be brave enough
to fight
for your smile,
along with someone else's joy.

One day,
your journey through loneliness
will end.

You must get out of your comfort zone.

And look for love
to find its way back to you.

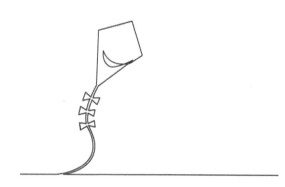

Rising

The Story of Youth

One day,
Life came back to me
with a story to say.

"I left you.
I was stupid.
I am sorry.
Can we be together again?"

This is the common story
of every teenager's life.
Mine included.
The story of heartbreaks,
self-discovery,
and love.

And the story went on like this
as I said,
"Oh, Dear *Life*,

"I felt so empty without you,
like a summer day without sun.
I am so sorry
that I let you go
and didn't ask you
for a second chance.
I was so weak
when I opened the door of my heart
and let you step out.
I am so sorry I never fought
to win you back.
All I have done these years
was to wait for you
to come back
and wake me up from death.
Oh, Dear *Life*,
I must tell you—
I was too weak as a teenager.
Weak and stupid.
I was too weak
to speak with you
and too stupid
to make a commitment with you."

But *Life* smiled at me
and replied,
"Oh, I know

how you felt,
for I felt the same way as you.
"I was unhappy
without you.
This is why I came back.
Can we start all over again?
I promise you
this time I will stay."

I bowed my head
and said,
"I promise you,
this time I will love you."

So this is my story.
And the common story
of every teenager's life.
The story of heartbreaks,
self-discovery, and love.
The story
of healing and growing.
The eternal story that goes on and on
until the end of time.

A Sensitive Heart

To stop feeling alone in a relationship,

you need a heart
which can handle your emotions
from a distance,
and hear your tears of longing
hitting the ground.

Cold

I am so cold.
Come closer to me.

Make room for me
in your heart.

Don't be afraid.

I want a warm shelter.

Melt your soul into my body.

Let a kiss slide down
to my heart.

Come closer.
Clothe me
with your body.

Warm me up
with your heart.

I want a cozy, safe shelter.
It is so painful
to be young and helpless.

Come closer.
I want you to love my heart.

Wipe away my fears
and dark thoughts.

Make my heart bloom again.
It is so hard for me
to be young
and in need of true love.

If You Are Heartbroken

If you are heartbroken,
don't cry too much.

Nothing good will happen.
Your pain will only grow
bigger and stronger
from your tears.

Wash your face,
step out of mourning,
and plant healing words
upon your heart's wounds.

One word at a time.

Nurture their roots
with hope.
Water them with light.

Let them bud.
Let them bloom.

One day,
you will have
a beautiful garden
filled with love's flowers.
And nobody will ever know
that your garden of light and love
was built
on the scattered pieces of your heart.

A Man Who Would Tell Me

I have always wanted
to meet a man
who would tell me,

"I love your heart's scars.

"I love your heart's wrinkles.
I love each and every one of them.
They are like giant waves
that you once climbed,
fought,
swam through,
rode,
and knocked down,
only to get to me.

"I love your entire aching heart
that witnessed
how tremendously you wanted
to meet me,
in this unfair world.
I love you."

Nothing Wrong

If someone breaks your heart,
let me tell you
that there is nothing wrong with you.
Sometimes,
people don't appreciate
someone who gives them
all the rivers of love.

You see,
nobody taught those people
good manners
and how to behave with love:
"Be honest, be kind, cherish,
respect, protect, heal,
believe, forgive, love."
They only muddle pure hearts.
And nobody taught you
that these people act like
thieves who steal

the innocence of a loving heart
only to throw it in the trash
like an apple core.
Nobody told you
that these people are sick,
for only sick people destroy love,
ruin hearts,
and tear apart innocence.
Nobody told you,
"Walk away from people
with unhealthy feelings
and immature souls.
They can't craft their lives
into something beautiful.
They can't love.
They can't offer you dignity.
Walk away from them."

I remind you,
there is nothing wrong with you.
It is just that nobody taught you
the immeasurable value
of your pure heart.
Nobody told you
how beautiful you are,
how worthy of love
you are.

You are a gem:
brilliant like a diamond,
and warm like a ruby.
Even if you are heartbroken now,
you still shelter a pure soul
inside your chest.
Even if you feel rejected now,
you nonetheless hunger for happiness,
for you are still innocent
and beautiful.
There is nothing wrong with you.
When you find true love,
you will look wonderful,
because your heart is already a pearl,
wanting to find a home
in the shell of happiness.

Gold

I am not afraid anymore.
All the fires that tried
to scorch my soul
didn't burn it to the ground,
but instead turned it into gold.

Now I know my worth.
I have discovered it
through the hell of suffering.

Your Time

If you say to yourself,
"I am sick of loneliness.
I am not useful to anyone,"
stop now.
Breathe.
Be patient!
You cannot
expect change to happen
or to receive happiness
all at once.
One day,
you will be cured.

Your time for love will come.

Our Society

We live in a society
filled with words,
but devoid of feelings.
Words spread everywhere
while genuine emotions are nowhere;
meaningful words get twisted,
but deep feelings are skeletons.

Don't be fooled.

Our hearts will break many times
while we live
in the shallowness of our world.

We should not give up though.
Let's be prepared to fight
and to protect our dreams.

Let's surround ourselves
with healthy hearts
to keep us company.

Don't let anyone prevent us
from believing
in the purity of love.
Don't let this society get in our way.

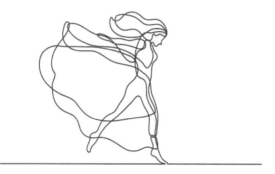

We must grow up
sensitive and powerful
at the same time.

Need to Bottle Up

One day,
you will not need
to bottle up your emotions
or freeze in your solitude.
You will wake up wishing
to take a walk,
to learn something beautiful,
to start a new life.

One day,
you will need
to cleanse your heart
like you would purge
a cluttered space.

One day,
you will yearn
to meet someone,
to give and receive an innocent smile.

One day,
you will triumph.
Loneliness will dissipate
like a cloud of smoke behind you.

The Hidden Paradise

Sometimes,
especially when you are sad,
you can't resist your wanderlust.
It is a strong desire
that distracts you from
your wounds
and makes you dream of
beautiful places
never before touched by pains,
never before corrupted by loneliness.
"Where are those wonderful places
where I can heal my heart?"

Don't look
on a map.

Don't search for a city.

Instead, touch your heart,
open the secret door
of your feelings,
step in the quiet inner world,
and look around.

Sometimes,
you have to visit your own heart
like a traveler goes to
a foreign country.

Sometimes,
you have to behave like a guest
with your feelings,
so that you can
lessen your melancholy.

Remember,
you are much more than your sadness.
You mean much more than your pain.

Go deep down inside your heart
and search for
the small and quiet place
where all the words come from love.

Some people named it
the Hidden Paradise.

Visit it,
catch a glimpse of its borders,
and kiss them.
You are safe here.

Now take your time
and learn
to make peace with yourself.
Then you can go anywhere,
for your heart will be healthy again.

A Special Beauty

If your heart is a garden,
one day
someone will open
the door to your feelings,
come in,
sit on a bench,
inhale the aroma of all your flowers,
and never want to leave.

One day
you will no longer be alone.

Until then,
you can do one thing.

Just plant a flower garden
of love and hope
in your heart.

Your Wings

If your heart breaks
and makes you crash in fear,
the first thing you need to heal
is the place
where your pain
ebbs and flows.

If you heal
that small, mysterious place
within your heart,
you will know
how to win back
your wings.

You Are an Eagle

Has anybody told you
that you are an eagle?

Has anybody told you
that you were born
to bring heaven
closer to this world?

You are a dreamer.

You don't need feathers
for your wings.

You already have
everything you need:
a whole brave heart
growing inside your chest.

Has anybody told you that?
Has anybody reminded you
that you can give birth to dreams
and noble ideals?

Or that you are meant for soaring?

My friend,
cut the ropes
that bind you
like a prisoner confined
to a cage.

Free yourself
from earthly thoughts.

Sever the leash
that tethers your freedom.

You are still raw,
innocent,
and wild.

You are an eagle.

Look at the sky's face.

Remember,
you were born to fly.

Don't Let Anyone

Don't let anyone
lead you to believe
that your heart will break
and you will lose
your glowing, innocent smile.

Don't let anyone lead you
to believe
that you will someday be defeated.

The blizzards of life
may slow you down
and even drop you to the ground.
But you will not be crushed.

Remember to whisper
in your hardest moments,
"I want to live.

"I want to get up.
I want to love and be loved.
I want to live."

Pull yourself up.

Don't let anyone
steal your confidence.

Remember that you may bend
like a reed
in the wind,
but never break.

You will not be defeated.

Into This Lonely World

How good it is to believe
that in this big lonely world
there is someone
made only for you,
someone
who can greatly comfort you,
someone
who can gently hold you,
someone
who truly wants
to fight for your heart.

How good it is to believe
that one day
you will meet that person.

How good it is to imagine
that one day

someone will tell you
with a warm voice,
"Let my heart become a home
for your love.
Let me be with you.
I love to be only with you.
I love the way we build
our happiness."

How good it is to believe
that one day,
all the pain
you feel right now
will be redeemed
through this true, beautiful love.

Changes

No matter how hard it would be,
no matter how much you'd ache
for relief,
there is only one way
to heal your broken heart.

Seek beauty
and transform it into
something bigger than yourself.
Make your life meaningful.
Don't sit alone and cry.

Your heart needs beauty
to stitch its wounds.

Reborn

"How can I escape from
the world of loneliness?"
you ask yourself.

This is a pointless sentiment,
for you were not meant
to carry
the burden of tough questions.

And you were not supposed
to run away
somewhere far
every day
to escape from the clutches
of loneliness.

Remember one thing.
Loneliness is akin to selfishness.

All you have to do is
stop focusing on yourself
to the point where
your vision of life
is the only one,
where your future
is all you can see,
or where your desires supersede
all others.

Be aware
that on this earth
there is something
more significant
than your loneliness.

So get out of your head,
forget your insecurities,
open your heart,
and make a friend—
a true friend,
not just someone to laugh with
during fair-weather times.
Go and help someone in need;
teach yourself to be meek,
good,
humble,

thankful,
caring,
and generous.

Wrap someone's heart
in softness,
sweetness,
and light.

Encourage yourself and others
to live
with kindness,
hope,
and purity.

If you do,
you will never worry
about being alone again,
for the deeds of love
will fill
your heart.

Giving

People talk a lot
about the illnesses of loneliness.
But no cure has been discovered
and every day people become
lonelier than ever.

You who read these verses,
please close this book
for a day or two,
and make time
for someone
who feels alone.
Pay a visit,
eat a cake together,
chat a little bit,
be meek,
gentle,
and humble.

Nobody needs the tyranny of pride.

Try to chase away
the ghosts of loneliness
with the peace of your kindness.

Before you leave,
seed a hug
in your friend's heart.

Nothing tastes better
than the honey of love.

The Weight of a Mountain

When I look into your eyes,
I can see so much sadness
that my heart rips apart.

"Where does this sadness come
from?"

Tell me.
I am here
with my heart
wide open.
Oh, if I could take your place,
I would carry
the weight
of your pains.
I would throw them away,
into a huge abyss,
never to be felt again.

If I could take your place,
I would cry out
your regrets
and your frustrations.
I would shed many tears.

Please, tell me
where it hurts.
I want to wipe away your sadness.

I want to mend your stricken heart.

I want to fight for your smile.

I want joy to build a nest
in your heart.

Sing, Dear Heart

You can feel small
like a hummingbird.

Yet your song is so powerful
and uplifting
that it fills the woods.

Sing, dear heart,
for you are not alone.

There are so many other hearts hidden
in the woods of this world.

They may be as slight as you
or tiny like every hummingbird.

Yet they are strong enough
to share their dreams
with the entire world.

Sing, dear heart.
Hope is meant to feed everyone.

Morning Questions

This morning I woke up
and asked myself,

"Where in this world
should I search for a healing word?"

I closed my eyes
and dreamed of you.

"Where are you,
my soul mate,
to love me,
to help me,
to strengthen my heart?"

I have no idea.

Although I do know
that dreaming of you
always eases
my aching heart
like a soft balm.

Last Night's Dream

Last night,
I had a strange dream.

It was like I had already met you.

We started to dance
until the world shrank
and turned into a walnut.

We were like a king and a queen
from a fairy tale,
owning everything.

When I woke up,
I held this dream in my heart
like a promise.

I knew that someday,
I would meet you.

Someday,
I will dance with you
until the whole world shrinks
and becomes a tiny walnut.

We will be king and queen
of our fairy tale.

Heal My Heart

I knew
you would heal and save me,
although I was heartbroken.
People always save
the ones they love.
And you loved me.

I knew
you would pour your kindness
over my wounds,
although I was heartbroken.
People always heal
the ones they love.
And you loved me.

I knew
you would cheer me up
when I lay my head

on your chest,
although I was heartbroken.
People always empower
the ones they love.
And you loved me.

I knew
you would make me happy again
when I believed in your love.
People always enrich
the ones they love.
And you loved me.

Healing Words

An old friend once taught me,
"Whenever you feel abandoned,
heartbroken, alone,
or when you are in need
of some healing words,
take a walk in the woods.
Look at the majestic trees around you,
and listen to the swish of leaves.
Lie down on the ground.
Look at the sky
through the canopy of branches.
Fully immerse yourself
in the peaceful surroundings.
Amid the silence,
listen carefully,
and the forest will share its secrets
for healing a broken heart."

And my friend continued speaking,
pretending to be the forest's voice,
"Hey, you,
look at me,
I have something to do every day.
I am busy blooming
and offering my beauties to the world.
I don't have time to be sad
when I lose trees or leaves.
I am full of enough seeds
waiting to embrace life
and to give away love.
Blooming and growing
are my daily duties."

Then my old friend hugged me,
"Don't let yourself be unsettled
by negative feelings.
Amid craziness,
you have to fight for your inner peace,
for your equilibrium."

And somehow
I heard the forest's voice in my heart.
"You are not perfect
and I am not perfect, either.
But this does not mean we are broken.

"You and I change daily.
You and I grow daily.
You and I understand
that life can't be constant daily.
You and I pass through
seasons of seeding,
seasons of growing,
seasons of blooming,
and seasons of withering.
And this is meant to teach us
that no season is eternal,
just like feeling sad or alone.
So next time when you feel abandoned,
heartbroken, or lonely,
or when you are in need of a healing word,
remind yourself that no season
can overcome your desire to bloom
and start all over again."

Live Like a Queen

There is only one way
to escape loneliness
and enjoy the abundance of life.
Love.

Choose love.

Give your heart
to those who respect
and love you back.

Devote yourself
to the unique beauty of love.
Live like a queen.
Live with generosity.
Live with a noble heart.
Live for love.
Live like a queen.

Choose love.
Love is the only season of life
whose beauty and light
never changes.
Choose love over being right.
Love over debates.
Love over being important.
Love over sadness.
Love over madness.
Love over anger.
Love over fears.
Love over tears.
Love over time.
Love.
Only love.

Dear Reader,

Thank you for reading my poetry collection. I hope my poems have resonated with you.

If you enjoyed this poetry book, the best way to show your appreciation is to spread the word. So please take a moment and leave a short review at the retailer's site where you purchased this book. Thank you very much.

I am grateful beyond words.

With love and poetry,
Alexandra

Acknowledgments

I am deeply grateful to God for guiding me in writing this poetry collection and helping me to understand that even tough life experiences are seasons of growth and self-healing. Only love and kindness open the doors to a life that brings and offers meaning.

Thanks also to my husband, who constantly encouraged and loved me with all his heart.

I am also grateful for the continued support and enthusiasm from my family, my friends, and my wonderful editor Chris—without her, this book couldn't have been possible.

Finally, I am also grateful and humbled at the same time to have so many beautiful readers who relate to my poems and anticipate more inspiring poetry books from me. Because of you, I had the courage to look deep into my heart and summon all the healing words that were living there innocently.

I hope that you will allow them to start a new life in your heart and comfort you whenever you need.

May my healing words accompany you in your soulful life experiences.

About the Author

Alexandra Vasiliu is an inspirational poet, and the bestselling author of *Healing Is a Gift*, *Healing Words*, *Time to Heal*, *Dare to Let Go*, *Be My Moon, Magnetic,* and *Blooming*.

Alexandra double majored in Literature and French for her undergraduate degree before pursuing her Ph.D. in Medieval Literature. When she isn't busy writing, she can be found browsing in bookstores, or spending time with her family at the beach.

Get in touch with her on Instagram @alexandravasiliupoetry and Facebook @AlexandraVasiliuWriter. Or visit her at alexandravasiliu.net. She loves hearing from her readers.